Publication of this book has been made possible by grants from the Devonian Group of Charitable Foundations, Calgary, Alberta, made to further knowledge of Canada's heritage and history, and from the Canada Council.

Portions of the text and illustrations are taken from *Haida Monumental Art: Villages of the Queen Charlotte Islands,* published by UBC Press with the support of the Devonian Group, the Government of British Columbia, and the B.C. Heritage Trust, and based on research funded by the National Museum of Man, National Museums of Canada, and the U.B.C. Museum of Anthropology.

Cover: Ninstints (Skungwa'ai) as it was in mid-nineteenth century. G. Miller
End papers: Haida frog emerging from whale's fluke (pole 7 x 1).

© The University of British Columbia Press 1983

Reprinted 1990

ISBN 0-7748-0163-8

Canadian Cataloguing in Publication Data

MacDonald, George F.
  Ninstints

(Museum note ; no. 12)
Bibliography: p.
ISBN 0-7748-0163-8

1. Ninstints (B.C.) - Antiquities. 2. Haida
Indians - Antiquities. I. University of British
Columbia. Museum of Anthropology. II. Title.
III. Series: Museum note (University of British
Columbia. Museum of Anthropology) ; no. 12.

E99.H2M33 1983   971.1'3100497   C83-091378-5

Museum Note Design: W. McLennan   Printed in Canada

Ninstints

Haida World Heritage Site

George F. MacDonald

Foreword by Michael M. Ames

Museum Note No. 12

University of British Columbia Press
in association with
the U.B.C. Museum of Anthropology

Vancouver

Fig. 1 Members of the 1957 expedition (from left, Wilson Duff, Harry Hawthorn, Bill Reid). BCPM (B. Atkins), 1957

Foreword

The Kunghit Haida of Ninstints are no more—they did not survive the onslaught of Western civilization. Their village, now only ruins, has been declared a World Heritage Site in memory of the cultivated society that once flourished there. But Ninstints is more than a celebrated relic; it provides as well a lesson in history and morals.

Dr. MacDonald describes in this book, and in his larger monograph *Haida Monumental Art*, how the Haida once lived, well endowed with both civility and pragmatism, their tempestuous and sometimes lucrative relations with the early European traders during the height of the maritime fur trade, and their great works of art and architecture. He also tells of the devastating impact of smallpox and other diseases introduced by Europeans that wiped out more than two-thirds of the Haida population and led to the abandonment of many villages like Ninstints.

Dr. MacDonald refers to recent efforts to preserve what remains of Ninstints. The 1957 expedition underwritten by Vancouver's Walter C. Koerner was probably one of the decisive turning points in this regard. The mapping of the village, archaeological excavations, and the careful preservation of some of the poles carried out in that year contributed significantly to a growing consciousness in our society of what had been lost. What was destroyed at Ninstints, and in other Indian villages along the British Columbia coast, was not just a few hundred lives. Wilson Duff and Michael Kew concluded in their report on the 1957 expedition:

Human beings must die anyway. It was something even more complex and even more human—a vigorous and functioning society, the product of just as long an evolution as our own, well suited to its environment and vital enough to participate in human cultural achievements not duplicated anywhere else. What was destroyed was one more bright tile in the complicated and wonderful mosaic of man's achievement on earth. Mankind is the loser. We are the losers.

Can the past ever be redeemed? The establishment of Ninstints as a World Heritage Site and the publication of scholarly works illustrating monumental Haida relics may count as modest beginnings, but there is something more important. The human cause is served little if, while preserving the past, we neglect the legitimate needs and aspirations of those who live today. If history has a lesson it is that the survivors are equally deserving of respect as any monument. The University of British Columbia Museum of Anthropology and its Shop Volunteers are therefore pleased to assist in the publication of this volume as a contribution to the future of the Haida and their land. We also express our appreciation to the Devonian Group of Charitable Foundations and the Leon and Thea Koerner Foundation for their support, and to the author for working to make the past more relevant.

Michael M. Ames
Director of the Museum of Anthropology

Fig. 2 Killer whale, mortuary pole 13 X 1.
BCPM (B. Atkins), 1957

Contents

Preface

The struggle between man's fragile efforts to create cultural monuments and nature's inevitable reclamation of those monuments is fascinating to behold, but it is usually so gradual it escapes our notice. There are but a few places in the world where this struggle between nature and culture is locked in a suspended state, where it is hard to say whether man or nature predominates. Most are in remote jungles and have such magic names as Ankor Wat or Ankor Thom in Cambodia, and Palenque or Chichen Itza, Mayan cities in the Yucatan Peninsula of Mexico. Ninstints is just this kind of site, although its jungle is of the high-latitude variety.

The forest at Ninstints isolates and obscures the monuments. The effect of the huge, severe faces of beavers and thunderbirds, exploded by the enormous roots of trees that are growing through them, is disturbing and memorable. Only glimpses of the faces and figures are caught as one moves through the standing trees and over the fallen ones blanketed in rich moss. Ninstints enjoys much sunny weather, at least during the summer, and throughout the day shafts of light cutting through the forest at varying angles spotlight the monuments in an ever-changing theatre of forest spirits.

The equation of nature and culture is never more sensationally expressed than at daybreak, when the low shafts of light coming over the eastern horizon plunge deep into the forest, picking out every remaining fragment of the art. The sun's first intense rays play over the precise curves and subtle planes of the Ninstints bestiary, which as a host peers towards the daybreak. Thick mats of moss carpet the tangled timbers of long collapsed houses. The isolating silence of Ninstints evokes a contemplative state — Ninstints is a natural cathedral where man and nature are perfectly balanced.

If a visitor to Canada were to ask me where the holiest of holy places of this country were to be found, I would be quick to respond that there are but three. One is the line of silent stone figures marching along the ridges that mark ancient shorelines of Pleistocene seas at Eskimo Point in the Northwest Territories. A second is the sculpture in glowing yellow cedar of "The Raven and the First Men," by Bill Reid, the Haida master carver, at the Museum of Anthropology at U.B.C. Last, but most impressive of all, is the village of Ninstints at daybreak when the raven's cry once more brings the world into being. Marius Barbeau (1954) caught the true significance of the achievement of the early Northwest Coast carvers:

Their genius has produced monumental works of art on a par with the most original the world has ever known. They belong one and all to our continent and our time, and have shown how creative power may thrive in remote places.

Fig. 3 Grizzly bear, mortuary pole 16 x 3. K. Spreitz, 1982

Introduction: The Kunghit Haida

The archaeological record indicates that people have inhabited the Queen Charlotte Islands for more than seven thousand years. At the time of the first contact with European explorers in 1775, there were an estimated six thousand Haida living in the Islands, and an additional three thousand living in the Prince of Wales Archipelago in southeast Alaska. These people spoke four dialects (Kunghit, Skidegate, Masset, and Kaigani) and occupied several dozen villages spread throughout their insular domain.

The Reverend William H. Collison, a missionary to the Haida in the latter years of the nineteenth century, described them thus (1915:90):
Many of the men were of fine physique, being six feet in stature; whilst those whose faces were not painted were much fairer in complexion than the Indians of the mainland. Some of their women wore nose-rings, and not a few of them were adorned also with anklets, whilst all the women wore silver bracelets, those of rank having several pairs, all carved with the peculiar devices of the respective crests.
By the late nineteenth century, all their numbers reduced drastically by European diseases, the Haida had abandoned all but two villages on the Queen Charlotte Islands, Masset and Skidegate. The huge ceremonial houses embellished with carved and painted clan emblems were completely deserted by 1880. Forest and climate soon reclaimed the monuments and structures so that today only photographs remind us of their splendour.

The southernmost group of Haida, who owned territories south of Lyell Island and had Ninstints as their main village, were known as the Kunghit Haida. Their remoteness had separated them linguistically from their northern neighbours, and John Swanton, an early ethnographer who visited the Haida at the turn of the century, claims they had (1909: 105): "considerable racial individuality. They were great fighters and sent expeditions in all directions."

The Kunghit Haida had about two dozen sizeable permanent villages scattered throughout their territory (Map 1). There were as well dozens more small settlements that were located near major resource areas and were occupied only for short periods each year. Hundreds of archaeological sites recorded by survey teams from Simon Fraser University testify to the fact that each stream that had a salmon run of any size had its own small settlement or camp on it.

Figs. 4 & 5 Sketches by Sigismund Bacstrom, March 1793, showing Haida of the southern Queen Charlottes. Note the pre-contact style canoe. Bacstrom comments that the cheeks of the chief and his wife were painted red. The woman wears a labret in her lower lip. PABC

The Sea pale Indigo over pencil waves, is best

/: East Side :/
Canoe with Indians at Port Rose, Queen Charlotte's Islands

In fant much lighter than the mother
mother's & fathers

Leave no white on
Face except the Str
Lights on the nose a
forehead

Hair Lak
and Chese
over pencil
then finishe
with the pe

do the principal
shades first with
the brush, then
the furr in p
then the pale
Transparent

Hatzia's Wife.

drawn after nature on friday 1 march 1793
on board of the 3 Bs
a dirty greenish - blue Cloak

N. 43

Hatzia   a Chief in Port Ro
South - End of Queen Charl: Isl
on the N. W. Coast of America

a Sea otter cloak - Sut brown m
with a little Lake

British Columbia

Queen
Charlotte
Islands

Moresby Island

20 Lyell Island

19

18

24

Ramsay Island

Juan Perez Sound

Hecate Strait

23

12

Gowgaia Bay

11

Burnaby Island

17

16

21
22

Skincuttle Inlet

15

14

Pacific Ocean

Carpenter Bay

13

10 9

Houston Stewart Cha

8

7

6 5

4

3 2

Anthony Island

Kunghit
Island

1

Cape St. James

Kerouard Islands

Map 1: The Kunghit Haida Region of
the Queen Charlotte Islands

1. Sqai
   family: Those Born at Songs of Victory Town
   chief: "Master of the Fire"

2. Xe-uda'o ("the village that always fishes towards the south")
   family: Those Born at Songs of Victory Town
   chief: "Raven"

3. Si'ndas Kun ("village on a point which is always smelling")
   family: Those Born at Songs of Victory Town
   chief: not recorded

4. Ła'gi
   family: Those Born at Songs of Victory Town
   chief: not recorded

5. Sga'ngwa-i ("red cod island town") or Ninstints
   family: Those Born up the Inlet
   chief: "He who is two"

6. Q'adadja'ns (ref. to a person who is annoyed with someone else and talks behind their back)
   family: Striped Town People
   chief: "Juicy grass"

7. Tcu'uga ("to go for cedar village")
   families: Those Born at Songs of Victory Town and Those Born in the Southern Part of the Islands
   chief: "Thunderbird"

8. Łgada'n (ref. to someone who tries to surpass another, and will suffer from it)
   family: Powerless Town People
   chief: not recorded

9. Sl'i'ndagwa-i ("the village deep in the inlet")
   family: Striped Town People
   chief: "Hawk feathers"

10. Na'gas ("town inhabited")
    family: Striped Town People
    chief: "Dead fish drifted ashore by the waves"

11. Tcuq'e-u ("mouth of the tide village")
    family: Those Born up the Inlet
    chief: "One without entrails"

12. Sqi'lgi (poss. "town where there are plenty of scoter ducks")
    family: Those Born up the Inlet
    chief: "He who is two"

13. Qai'dju ("Songs of Victory Town")
    family: Sand Town People
    chief: Kia'nskina-i

14. Ga'idi ("smelt village")
    family: Sand Town People
    chief: Kia'nskina-i

15. Xa'gi
    family: Striped Town People
    chief: Wada (a type of clam)

16. La'na da'gana ("badtalk village")
    family: Those Born up the Inlet
    chief: Gitkun

17. Q'et ("Narrow Strait Village")
    family: Narrow Strait Town People
    chief: "Making a copper sound by lying upon it"

18. Ata'na
    family: Sand Town People
    chief: Kia'nskina-i

19. Ga-isiga's q'eit ("strait town where no waves come ashore")
    family: Striped Town People
    chief: "Raven's bones"

20. Xo'tdjixoa's ("hair seal low tide town")
    family: Striped Town People
    chief: Gi'tiqo'na-i

21. Qai'djudal
    family: Slaves
    chief: "Always ready for anything"

22. La'na xa'wa ("swampy village)
    no details recorded

23. Gado'
    no details recorded

24. Gaiega'n kun
    no details recorded

The larger Kunghit Haida villages had a half-dozen or more houses, each home to thirty to forty individuals. Population ranged from less than two hundred to more than five hundred. Each village usually included families from different lineages of the Ravens and Eagles, the two groups, or moieties, into which the Haida divided their people in order to regulate inter-marriage and the succession of rights and property. The village chief was always from the dominant or founding lineage. Each village controlled a salmon breeding stream, offshore fishing grounds for black cod and halibut, and inter-tidal collecting areas for shellfish, as well as some hunting and gathering areas on the islands.

John Swanton describes the way in which the Haida spent their days (1909: 71):

When spring came, the people abandoned their towns and scattered to camp, where the men fished for halibut, salmon, and on the West Coast for black cod, and hunted black bear, marten, seals, sea-lions, etc.; while their wives picked berries, dug roots, and cultivated a patch of tobacco, their only agricultural labor. Each Haida family had its own creek, creeks, or portion of a creek, where its smoke-houses stood. Some of the smaller creeks are said to have had no owners; and, on the other hand, some families are said to have had no land. In the latter case they were obliged to wait until another family was through before picking berries, and had to pay for the privilege. Any family might pick berries on the land belonging to another after the owners had finished picking, if it obtained the consent of the latter and paid a certain price.... Near each of the towns was a place used by the children for a play-ground. There they often took their lunches and spent the whole day.

In the winter, the season of short days and wild storms in the exposed Kunghit region, the Haida engaged in ritual and ceremony, visiting and en-tertaining the inhabitants of other villages, feasting on the foods that they had dried and pre-served from the summer's plenty.

Fig. 6 Crests depicting the two moieties of the Haida: eagle (top) and raven (below). (House 13, frontal pole) BCPM (C.F. Newcombe), 1901

Ninstints: The Village

Anthony Island is a relatively small island exposed to the sweep of the open Pacific. However, the village site of Ninstints is the most secluded and protected of all major Haida villages, since it is located in a sheltered bay on the eastern side of the island and is further protected by a rocky islet facing the village. There is a single, narrow, navigable channel to the south of the islet providing access to the sheltered bay at high tide. At low tide the bay is completely dry. On the islet was a small fortification which served as a refuge in times of war. Burials were common on the islet, including small grave houses and shaman graves.

The name "Ninstints" was a corruption by Europeans of the name of the head chief of the village, *Nañ stins* ("He who is two"). The Haida name for the village was *Sqa'ngwa-i lnaga'i*, Red Cod Island Town. It was probably this town that John Work, in a census of Haida villages conducted in 1840–41, referred to as *Quee-ah*, after an earlier chief, *Koyah* ("Raven"). Work said the village had twenty houses and a population of 308. Swanton (1909: 282) also lists details for twenty houses which were provided to him in 1900 by a daughter of the Ninstints who had been chief of the village at the time of its abandonment.

Fig. 7 Reconstruction of the southern end of the village in the mid-nineteenth century. G. Miller, UBCMOA

Fig. 8 Mortuary pole 15 x 2, showing some crests of Koyah's people: the moon and the thunderbird. BCPM (C.F. Newcombe), 1901

The Eagle families of the Kunghit Haida at Ninstints included Those Born up the Inlet, which was the ruling family of the village during the half-century before it was abandoned; Those Born in the Southern Part of the Islands and two related lineages, the Powerless Town People and the Stagi Town People; the Djigua Town People; and the Pebble Town Eagles. The Kunghit Raven families were fewer in number, although in Ninstints they occupied almost the same number of houses as the Eagles. They included the Striped Town People; the Sand Town People; and the family which ruled Ninstints at the time of first contact with Europeans, Those Born at Songs of Victory Town.

The main house row at Ninstints straddled a natural terrace bordering the bay. The northern end was bounded by a low marshy area, and the southern end opened onto a small meadow. The front row of houses was broken by the line of the beach. Wilson Duff and Michael Kew (1958: c47) assume that the terrace was the preferred area for houses, but once the terrace sites had been occupied, expansion of the village had to take place in a new row of houses, in front of the terrace, at the northern and southern ends of the village. Swanton (1909: 282–83) distinguishes the two rows only at the southern end of the village, merging them together at the northern end.

The houses associated with the last few generations of chiefs bearing the name Ninstints were at the southern end of the town (Houses 1, 3, 4, and 5). It is interesting to note that the house at the northern end of the village (House 17) is called by Swanton's informant *Xo'ya na'as*, or Koyah's House (or "Raven House"). In addition, one of the mortuaries (15x2) standing in front of House 15 bears the moon and the thunderbird, crests of Koyah's people, Those Born at Songs of Victory Town, although neither the house nor the monuments appear to date back as far as the Chief Koyah referred to by the traders.

Fig. 9 The northern end of the village.
G. Miller, UBCMOA

The southern section of Ninstints, Houses 1–7, was dominated but not exclusively inhabited by Eagle lineages, and included the house of the head chief, Ninstints. In the northern section, Houses 8–17, the northern and southern-most houses have elaborate frontal poles and carved interior poles. One of the central houses, House 12, is situated on a high terrace and has an excavated interior pit. Three of the houses were known to have carved interior poles but no house pits. Although it may not be significant, they stood at the two extremities and the middle of the village (Houses 1, 8, and 17).

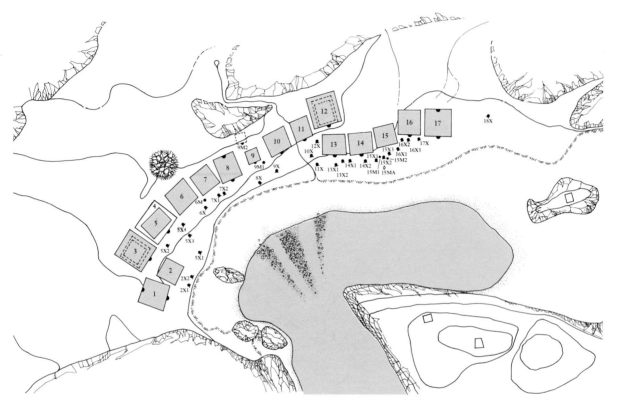

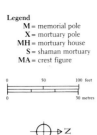

Map 2: Houses in the Village

House 1. People Think of This House Even When They Sleep Because the Master Feeds Everyone Who Calls

House 2. Cloudy House

House 3. Thunder Rolls upon it House

House 4/5. Grease House

House 6. House That Is Always Shaking

House 7. No name recorded

House 8. No name recorded

House 9. No name recorded

House 10. People Wish to be There House

House 11. Driving a Weasel House

House 12. Mountain House

House 13. No name recorded

House 14. No name recorded

House 15. No name recorded

House 16. No name recorded

House 17. Raven House

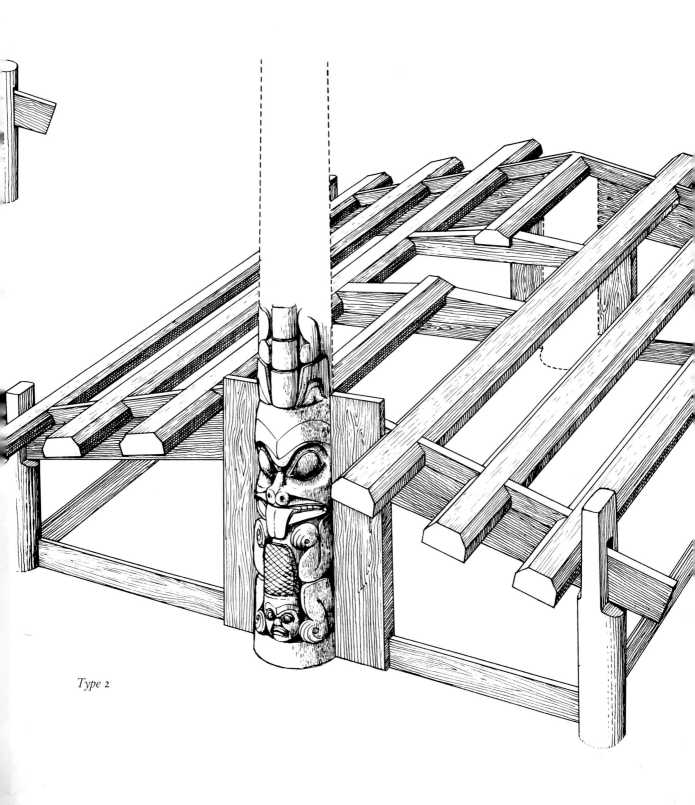

Type 2

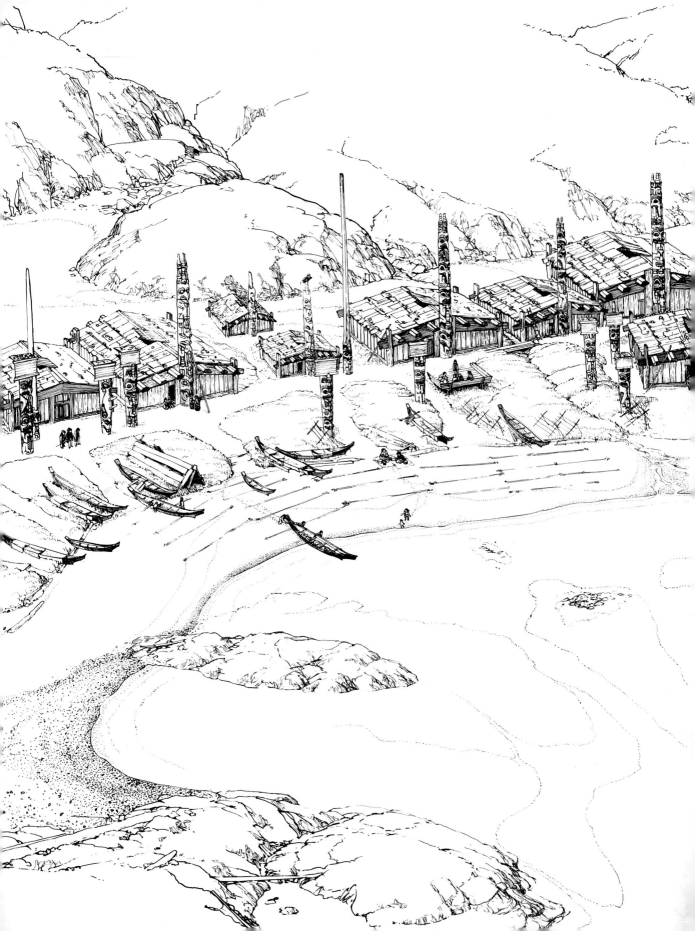

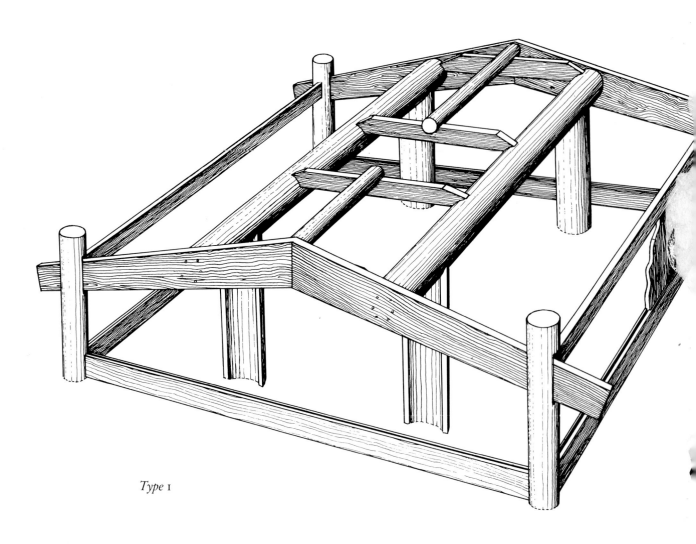

Type 1

Fig. 10 *Line drawing of the village of Ninstints, based upon archaeological research, C.F. Newcombe's 1901 photographic records, and observation on the site. G. Miller, UBCMOA*

Houses in the Village

The Haida built two types of houses, which differed mainly in the approach to construction, rather than in the character of the finished house. Type 1 is a simple support structure of two parallel round beams set on pairs of uprights. To this basic structure is added a framework of light rafters, sills, corner posts, and gables, which is then covered with planks. There is little integration between massive frame and light covering.

House type 2 integrates all the structural members and distributes the stress by employing more elaborate joinery, including mortice-and-tenon joints and interlocking features. The sheeting is further integrated into the frame by joinery. The extensive use of joinery in this type of house, with supports integrated into the walls, adds structural strength and provides more interior space.

The most radical difference between the two types is in the gables or barge boards which in type 2 houses must carry the heavy weight of the six longitudinal rafters. The thickness of the gables was increased towards the apex for added strength.

Among other tribes on the Northwest Coast, all houses are of type 1. Furthermore, an eighteenth-century drawing of Kiusta shows only type 1 houses. Among the Haida, distribution of type 2 houses ranges from almost none in the Alaskan villages of the Kaigani Haida to an overwhelming majority in the southern villages. This suggests that type 1 was the original form of house construction and that the type 2 style was a specialized later development which originated in the southern villages. It is likely that type 2 house construction originated at Ninstints. All of the earlier houses there were of this type, although some simpler structures were used to replace them in the late period of occupation.

Figs. 11 & 12 Haida house types: type 2 was the dominant style at Ninstints.
G. Miller, UBCMOA

It is interesting to speculate that the development of the type 2 house was spawned by the introduction of European iron tools and techniques of joinery to the Haida by ships' carpenters. There are suggestions from other parts of the Pacific basin, including Indonesia, that as a part of cargo cult religious beliefs that arose to explain the sudden arrival of European explorers, native house styles shifted towards the emulation of trading ships and galleons. It is possible that the creation of the type 2 style among the Haida arose from a similar impulse.

Fig. 13 Decayed rear corner post and structural beams of House 12. BCPM (A. Hoover), 1971

Fig. 14 *Aerial photograph of a section of southern Anthony Island, showing the sheltered village site of Ninstints with its narrow entrance channel and rocky burial islet offshore. B.C. Ministry of Environment, 1980*

Fig. 15 *House 1 frontal pole, depicting a beaver. UBCMOA (H.Hawthorn), 1957*

When a high-ranking chief had accumulated the wealth required to raise a house, he contracted with people of the opposite moiety to assemble the materials. The selected work parties set out in groups of thirty to forty in five-or-six-man canoes to the cutting site. All would paddle strongly with an accompaniment of songs in time with the paddle-strokes, led by the man in the bow.

The site selected for cutting timbers was either one recognized as belonging to the family of the chief building the house or one for which the privilege to cut timbers had been acquired by payment to another family. If possible, a site was selected where the timber was near the water, so the canoes could be brought in or where a minimum of skidding was required. On an earlier reconnaissance of the area, the chief had selected the particular trees to be cut. Newcombe states: *On landing at the selected place a fire was made as near the centre of operation as possible, and here the chiefs sat and directed the work as it went on. As the winter months were always chosen, these fires were used, not only for this reason but also for the heating of vast quantities of food provided by the women.*

Once cut, the logs were floated and towed back to the village, where they were barked and split into planks or beams. Then the house was constructed with great care and precision. The final act, accompanied by a potlatch to celebrate the completion of the house, was the erection of the carved frontal pole, which bore the crests earned or inherited by the house family.

Fig. 16 Top of interior post, House 1.
UBCMOA (B. McLennan), 1983

Fig. 17 Mortuary posts 7x1 & 7x2 (foreground).
BCPM (C.F. Newcombe), 1901

Figs. 18 & 19 The details of the crests of mortuary post 2x1 have been deduced from comparison with crests of unburned poles.
B.C. Ministry of Tourism, 1980   *G. Miller*

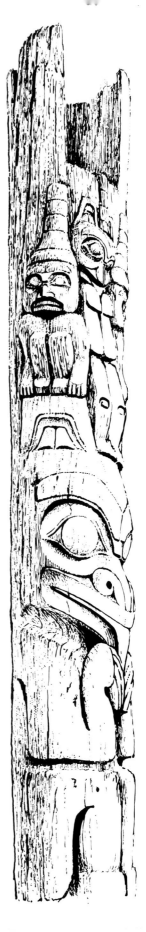

17

Fig. 20 *Although burnt almost beyond recognition, the crests of mortuary post 5x2, a bear and a killer whale, still project a powerful presence. B.C. Ministry of Tourism, 1980*

Fig. 21 *Mortuary post 7x1, a double-finned killer whale. V. Husband, 1982*

Fig. 22 *Frog protruding from under the killer whale's fin. V. Husband, 1982*

Fig. 23 Mortuary poles (foreground) 7x1 & 7x2. Note the small figures which adorn the larger crests, such as the watchman figures at the base of 7x2, the face on the tail of the beaver above, and the frog between its arms. NMC (C.M. Barbeau), 1947

Figs. 24 & 25 *View from south end looking north. Frontal poles for Houses 8 & 9 are to the right of Plate 24. BCPM (C.F. Newcombe), 1901*

Fig. 26 *Base of House 9 frontal pole now at the UBC Museum of Anthropology. UBCMOA (B. McLennan), 1983*

Fig. 27 *Interior post, House 8. The human figure is a chief wearing a dance hat and holding a talking stick. BCPM (C.F. Newcombe), 1913*

Fig. 28 *Top of mortuary pole* 13XI.
UBCMOA (H. Hawthorn), 1957

Fig. 29 *View of Ninstints.*
UBCMOA (H. Hawthorn), 1957

Fig. 30 *Mortuary poles. K. Spreitz*, 1982

Fig. 31 *Memorial pole* 9M2 *depicted a killer whale with its tall dorsal fin at top and a grizzly bear at base. BCPM (C.F. Newcombe),* 1913

Fig. 32 *Looking north. BCPM (C.F. Newcombe),* 1901

Fig. 33 *Frontal poles for Houses* 10, 11 *&* 13, *and associated mortuaries. BCPM (C.F. Newcombe),* 1901

Fig. 34 *Detail of hand and frog from House 9 frontal pole. UBCMOA (H. Hawthorn), 1957*

Fig. 35 *Remains of a house frame. UBCMOA (H. Hawthorn), 1957*

Fig. 36 *The last living evidence of horticulture at Ninstints – a domestic apple tree. B.C. Ministry of Tourism, 1980*

Fig. 37 *Fragment of a ceramic plate from London's Crystal Palace, excavated at Ninstints. BCPM (B. McLennan), 1983*

Fig. 38 Frontal pole of House 12 (rear) and frontal pole and mortuary (13x1) of House 13. Note human legs protruding from mouth of grizzly bear at the base of the House 13 frontal pole. BCPM (C.F. Newcombe), 1901

Fig. 39 Base section of House 12 frontal pole, now at UBC Museum of Anthropology. The main crest is a bear, with a frog in its mouth, a wolf between its legs, and a cub between its ears. UBCMOA (B. McLennan), 1983

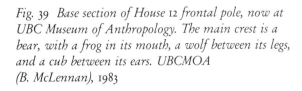

Fig. 40 *Site reconstruction drawing of House 12, showing frontal pole and mortuary (12X). G. Miller, UBCMOA*

Fig. 41 *A modern house frontal pole carved by Bill Reid, assisted by Douglas Cranmer, based on the House 12 frontal pole. UBCMOA (B. McLennan), 1983*

Fig. 42 *Mortuary post 14x2, depicting an eagle.*
(C.F. Newcombe), 1901

Fig. 43 *The same pole, forty-six years later, showing*
the deterioration caused by the environment.
NMC (C.M. Barbeau), 1947

Fig. 44 *House 14 frontal pole and mortuaries. The*
central crest on the frontal pole is a fat frog with five
potlatch rings emerging from its head. The rings
simultaneously form the frog's backbone and an
image of the world axis, sometimes figured as the
backbone of an ancestor. BCPM (B. Atkins), 1957

Fig. 45 (left) Mortuary pole 15x1, showing a sea grizzly holding a seal. BCPM (B. Atkins), 1957

Fig. 46 Poles associated with Houses 15 & 16. BCPM (C.F. Newcombe), 1913

Fig. 47 The same poles, looking north, with House 17 frontal pole in the background and mortuary 18x to the right. BCPM (C.F. Newcombe), 1901

Fig. 48 *Mortuary poles associated with Houses 15 &* *16. The small, free-standing sculpture (or* manda) *to* *the left depicts a grizzly bear. BCPM(C.F.Newcombe),* 1913

Fig. 49 *Reconstruction drawing, based on Fig. 48,* *shows this part of the village as it might have been in* *the late nineteenth century before abandonment.* *G. Miller, UBCMOA*

Fig. 50 Detail of the back of pole 15x2, showing whale's fluke. Pole now at the UBC Museum of Anthropology. UBCMOA (B. McLennan), 1983

The crests carved on the frontal poles, and on memorial and mortuary poles erected to honour the dead, represented animals, both natural and supernatural, natural phenomena, such as cumulus and cirrus clouds or rainbows, as well as celestial bodies like the moon and the stars. At other times, items of Haida material culture are portrayed, such as war helmets or ermine-skin head-dresses. Whether of animal or other origin, all of these crests were shown in animal-like or manlike forms.

Ideally, each moiety should have had crests that were unique, which would have separated it clearly from the other. To some extent this was true, but some transfer of crests occurred between moieties on the north and south coasts. Not all families were entitled to use all of the crests that were the property of their moiety; crests were jealously guarded. According to Swanton (1909: 108):

if any chief learned that one of his crests had been adopted by a chief of a family that was considered of lower rank, he would put the latter to shame, and by giving away or destroying more property than the other chief could muster, force him to abandon it.

Through the potlatch new crests could be introduced to the system in the form of a mask, a tattoo design, or a house post motif, although the relatively limited number of Haida crests suggests that the amount of wealth needed to buy, or honour needed to bestow, a new crest was quite large.

Fig. 51–53 Mortuary poles 15x2, 15x3, 16x2 & 16x3. NMC (C.M. Barbeau), 1947

Fig. 54 (left) Frontal pole for House 17.
BCPM (B. Atkins), 1957

Fig. 55 Base of the pole showing grizzly bear
devouring a human being. The house entrance is
carved through the stomach of the bear.
NMC (C.M. Barbeau), 1947

Fig. 56 Detail showing human being wearing a skirt
formed of five inverted figures and holding two
smaller figures. The nose of the large human figure has
been slotted to receive an attachment.
UBCMOA (H. Hawthorn), 1957

Fig. 57 *Interior post at back of House 17, now at the UBC Museum of Anthropology. The figure at the top is a human embracing a hawk and a bear cub; at the base is a bear embracing a human. Small frogs emerge from the bear's ears.*
BCPM (C.F. Newcombe), 1901

Fig. 58 *Detail of House 17 interior post.*
UBCMOA (B. McLennan), 1983

Fig. 59 *(right) Mortuary post 18x2, depicting grizzly bear and human infant.* BCPM (B. Atkins), 1957

Fig. 60 *Reconstruction drawing of a Haida house interior, based on early accounts. G. Miller*

Life inside the house centred on the open central hearth, where a fire was always burning for warmth and for the preparation of meals. This hearth was also the focus for any ceremonies held in the house.

Sleeping compartments were erected according to the rank of the occupant, beginning with the chief's compartment at the centre back of the house. Moveable furniture was rare, except for the chief's seat, which was a legless bench that on ceremonial occasions was set in the place of honour at the centre of the back of the house. In their journal, published in 1801, Captain Chanal and Surgeon Roblet provide the following description of the interior of a house at Dadens, a village located at the northwest tip of the Queen Charlotte Islands:

The fire is placed in the middle of the edifice; there it is that the food is dressed. This same apartment fifty feet long, serves at once, for kitchen, dining-room, bed chamber, stove house, and workshop, and also as a shed for the canoe, when she is not employed afloat. While on one side, some women are giving
their attention to the children and to the family concerns, some, elsewhere, are drying and smoking fish for the winter stock; and others are busied in making mats, and joining and sewing furs in order to make them into cloaks. No fixed places were distinguishable for sleeping, and according to appearances, all the individuals of a family sleep pell-mell on the boarded floor of the habitation.... But if they are so negligent with respect to themselves, they are less so in regard to their children: the youngest are laid in cradles suspended like hammocks. Our voyageurs saw a considerable number of chests piled up on the sides and in the corners of the habitation, and they learnt that these chests hold the winter provisions, and that, in others, are contained bows and arrows. In different places on the walls, were hung darts, lances, nets, fish-hooks, with poles and lines for fishing. The habitations are, in general, painted and decorated in various ways.

Early Contact with Europeans

Ninstints is the earliest recorded Haida town of the southern Queen Charlotte Islands, and it is mentioned in ship's logs from the early sea otter trade. On 24 July 1787, George Dixon, in his ship, the *Queen Charlotte,* encountered eleven canoes of Kunghit Haida off Anthony Island, who were evidently already accustomed to the idea of trade with Europeans, since they showed no fear and brought skins to trade.

The first description of Ninstints is provided by Robert Haswell in the log of the *Lady Washington,* commanded by Captain Robert Gray, for June 1789 (Howay 1941: 97):

A brisk trade was soon set on foot by Coya the chief, who bartered for all his subjects. . . . I landed to take an excursion in the woods when I met with a fortified rock which I suppose in case of invasion is their place of refuge. It was perpendicular, about forty feet high. The top was flat; about twenty yards wide. It was inaccessible on all sides except by an old rotten ladder that was erected by its side. This fort they called touts and when their northern neighbours come to molest them they put their women and children up there while they fight the battle.

Although the first visit of the *Lady Washington* resulted in amicable trade, later in 1789, when the ship returned under the command of John Kendrick, hostility grew between the Kunghit Haida and the white traders. Pilfering of minor items from the ship led to a violent and irrational reaction. The incident that triggered open hostility was the theft of the captain's laundry, which had been hung out to dry aboard ship. Kendrick ordered the two chiefs, Koyah and Skulkinanse, seized, and he held them as hostages until his clothes were returned.

Although all but a few items were returned, he forced the chiefs to have their remaining furs brought aboard and sold at a price he determined. Captain Gray, on a later visit to the area, added further details of the incident from native accounts. The Ninstints people claimed that Captain Kendrick (Howay 1941: 200):

took Coyah, tied a rope around his neck, whipped him, painted his face, cut off his hair, took away from him a great many skins, and then turned him ashore. Coyah was now no longer a chief, but an 'Ahliko', or one of the lower class. They now have no head chief, but many inferior chiefs.

Fig. 61 Encounter between Haida in their canoes and the crew of the Lady Washington, *an early trading vessel. G. Miller*

In June 1791, Captain Kendrick returned to trade at Ninstints. The captain had been drinking and allowed at least fifty Indians on board to trade without arming his crew. Koyah seized the keys to the arms chest and forced the crew below decks (Howay 1925: 293):

The vessel was immediately thronged with natives, a woman standing in the main rigging urging them on. The officers and people all retired below, having no arms but what was in possession of the natives, save the officers' private ones. Captain Kendrick tarried on deck endeavoring to pacify the natives and bring them to some terms, at the same time edging towards the companion way to secure his retreat to the cabbin, a fellow all the time holding a huge marling spike he had stolen, fixed into a stick, over his head, ready to strike the deadly blow whenever orders should be given. The other natives with their daggers grasped and only waiting for the word to be given to begin a most savage massacre. Just as Captain Kendrick had reached the companion way Coyah jumpt down and he immediately jumpt on top of him. Coyah then made a pass at him with his dagger, but it luckily only went through his jacket and scratched [him]. The officers by this time had their arms in readiness and would have ventured on deck with them before but for fear of killing their captain. Captain Kendrick now fired a musket from the cabbin, then took a pair of pistols and another musket and went on deck, being followed by his officers with the remainder of the arms they had collected. The natives on seeing this made a precipitate retreat, all but the woman before mentioned in the chains who there continued urging them to action with the greatest ardour until the last moment though her arm had been previously cut off by one of the people with a hanger and she was otherwise much wounded. When she quitted all the natives had left the vessel and she jumped over board and attempted to swim off but she was afterwards shot. Though the natives had taken the keys of the arm chests yet they did not happen to be lockt. They were therefore immediately opened and a constant fire was kept up as long as they could reach the natives with the cannon or small arms. After which they chased them in their armed boats, making the most dreadful havock by killing all they came across.

This incident was immortalized in a sea shanty, probably composed by one of the crew, which was popular among the New England traders for decades afterwards (Howay 1929: 115–17):

BOLD NORTHWESTMAN

Come all ye bold Northwestmen who plough the raging main,
Come listen to my story, while I relate the same;
'Twas of the Lady Washington decoyed as she lay,
At Queen Charlotte's Island, in North America.

On the sixteenth day of June, boys, in the year Ninety-One,
The natives in great numbers on board our ship did come,
Then for to buy our fur of them our captain did begin,
But mark what they attempted before long time had been.

Abaft upon our quarter deck two arm chests did stand,
And in them there was left the keys by the gunner's careless hand;
When quickly they procuring of them did make a prize,
Thinking we had no other arms for to defend our lives.

Our captain spoke unto them and unto them did say,
If you'll return me back those keys I for the same will pay;
No sooner had he spoken these words than they drew forth their knives,
Saying the vessels ours sir, and we will have your lives.

Our captain then perceiving the ship was in their power,
He spoke unto his people, likewise his officers,
Go down into the cabin and there some arms prepare,
See that they are well loaded, be sure and don't miss fire.

Then with what few fire arms we had we rush'd on deck amain,
And by our being resolute, our quarter deck we gain'd;
Soon as we gain'd our arm chest such slaughter then made we,
That in less than ten minutes our ship of them was free.

Then we threw overboard the dead that on our deck there lay;
And found we had nobody hurt, to work we went straightway;
The number kill'd upon our deck that day was sixty good,
And full as many wounded as soon we understood.

'Twas early the next morning at the hour of break of day,
We sail'd along abreast the town which we came to straightway;
We call'd on hands to quarters and at the town did play,
We made them to return what things they'd stolen that day.

I'd have you all take warning and always ready be,
For to suppress those savages of Northwest America;
For they are so desirous some vessel for to gain,
That they will never leave it off, till most of them are slain.

And now unto old China we're fastly rolling on,
Where we shall drink good punch for which we've suffered long;
And when the sixteenth day of June around does yearly come,
We'll drink in commemoration what on that day was done....

To avenge their humiliation, the Ninstints chiefs led raids on passing ships. One was on an unidentified English ship that put into Ninstints harbour for repairs sometime in 1794, where she was attacked with the loss of all hands. Another was on an American ship, probably the *Eleanora*, under the command of Captain Simon Metcalfe. In this episode, there was one survivor whose fate is recorded in the log of the *Ruby* (Howay 1925: 296–98):

some time in the year '94 Capt. Metcalf came to an anchor in his Brig at Coyar's Sound & began a friendly traffic for furs with the Savages, but not being much suspicious of them, let a great number come upon his decks & the natives taken advantage of their superiority in numbers, clinch'd and stab'd, ev'ry man on board, except ye one that sprung up the Shrouds. This horrid Massacre was executed in the space of a few minutes with no loss, on the side of the natives. The man said that after they had insulted the body's of ye dead as they thought sufficiently, they told him to come down, which he accordingly did & deliver'd himself up to them, at the same time begging for mercy. They immediately took him on shore at the Village, where he was kept in the most abject slavery for about a twelve month. In the winter & in the worst of weather amidst Snow & ice, they would drive him into ye Woods, to fetch logs & when he had got most to ye Village with his load, he would be met, by his task masters, who would disburthen him & drive him back after more & when any Vessell came into the harbour they would lash him hand & foot to a tree & keep him in that situation with a scanty allowance till she again sail'd for fear that he might run away.

The last attack was on the ship *Union* under Captain John Boit on 21 June 1795. It was lead by the head chief of the area, Scorch Eye, or "Skoich-eye" (Howay 1925: 301).

Above 40 Canoes Came into the Cove, full of Indians, at least 300 men. I immediately suspected by their manoeuvres that they meant to attack the Union. Call'd all hands to quarters. Eight chiefs were on board at this time who began to be very saucy & the war Canoes kept pressing alongside, & the Indians geting upon the Nettings. Scorch Eye the head chief began the attack by seizing Mr. Hudson, the 2nd officer. At the same time the Indians along side attempted to board, with the most hideous yells. However we soon paid them for their temerity. I killed their first Chief, Scorch Eye, in the 2nd mates arms, while they was struggling together. The rest of the Chiefs on board was knock'd down & wounded & we kill'd from the Nettings & in the Canoes along side above 40 more when they retreated, at which time I could have kill'd 100 more with my grape Shot, but I let humanity prevail & ceas'd firing. At 6 P.M. a Small Canoe came off, from the village with 2 Indians in her holding Green bows (Emblems of Peace). I allowed the Chiefs on board, who was thoroughly Iron'd to hold converse with them. At dark they left us. Kept a Strong watch, all hands to quarters through the night.

At daylight [on the 22nd] took up the anchors and came to sail, stretching towards the Village on the West part of the Sound. At 9 A.M. seviall large Canoes put off full of Indians waving green bows. They came along side with fear & trembling, bringing plenty of furs to ransom their Chiefs with. Order'd the Irons of them & call'd the poor deivils up, & notwithstanding the treatment I'd receiv'd I paid full price for the Skins. Believe I got every piece of fur they had in the village. Took notice that the Village was deserted. Suppose they thought it was our intention to destroy itt. At 11 A.M. the Canoes left us the Indians crying & praying for our success. Indeed the treatment they rec'd from me was quite different from what they expected. Suppose in this fracas we kill'd & wounded about 50 but the Indians said we killed 70. None of us was hurt, but their attack was very impolitic, for had they instead of being so intent to board, stood off & fir'd their Arrows, no doubt they would have kill'd & wounded seviall of us. However I was too well guarded against supprize, for them to have been victorious.

There is no doubt that the Kunghit Haida, especially under the direction of Koyah, were a warlike people—in some ways this was a necessary quality to ensure their survival in their rugged environment. However, this attribute should not be overstressed. The words of trader William Sturgis, contradicting the opinion of an early historian, provide a more balanced view (Howay 1925: 309):

He ascribes it (Indian violence towards traders) to the treachery and ferocity of the Indians; I, with better opportunities for investigating and ascertaining the truth, find the cause in the lawless and brutal violence of white men; and it would be easy to show that these fatal disasters might have been averted by a different treatment of the natives and by prudence and proper precaution on the part of their civilized visitors.

Over the decades that followed, relations between the Kunghit Haida and the white settlers improved. Although depleted stocks and declining demand reduced the impact of the fur trade on their lives, the Haida became increasingly involved with European goods and European ways through their participation as wage labourers in the new resource industries of mining and logging. Many moved to the larger villages of Masset and especially Skidegate where they would have easier access to this new economy, and some even travelled as far as Victoria, on southern Vancouver Island, in search of jobs.

The downfall of Ninstints did not come at the hands of a human enemy, but was the result of the accidental introduction of smallpox. In December of 1863, Francis Poole, who was mining at Skincuttle Inlet, notes in his narrative (1872: 194–95):

At New Aberdeen we had compassionately taken a European on board as a passenger via Queen Charlotte to Victoria. As ill luck would have it what should he do but fall sick of small-pox, some days before we arrived at the coppermines. I entered a vehement protest against his being put on shore,

knowing only too well the certain consequences. The little skipper insisted, however, and then weighed anchor without him. We whites, it is true, were not attacked [by smallpox]; but scarce had the sick man landed when the Indians again caught it; and in a very short space of time some of our best friends of the Ninstence or Cape St. James tribe... had disappeared forever.

In the next ten years, Ninstints was visited by a series of epidemics, which proved fatal to many of the villagers. By 1875 it was used only as a camp. As with most Haida villages it is difficult to establish an exact date for the abandonment, but George M. Dawson, a federal government geographer, states that it was abandoned by the time of his visit in 1878. When Newton H. Chittenden visited the Islands on a mineral survey for the provincial government in 1884, there were thirty former inhabitants camped at the village. The houses and monuments fell into ruins, and about 1892 several of them at the southern end of the village were burned by Koskimo Indians and the crew of a sealing schooner.

Tom Price: The Last Ninstints

We tend to think of Ninstints as a collection of monuments of superhuman scale and yet there is a legacy of that village on a much more human scale in terms of the many tools, utensils, ceremonial paraphernalia and other such artifacts that now reside on shelves and in exhibit cases of museums around the world. This part of the research on Ninstints has yet to be done. Some of these artifacts were taken by survivors to Skidegate village where descendants sold them to the scores of collectors who combed the village for Haida artifacts over the past century. Other pieces were removed from abandoned houses and stolen from burial caves and mortuaries at Ninstints. Many of these pieces have lost their recorded link to Ninstints, others have been merely forgotten in museum storage rooms. We do know that through collectors like Charles F. Newcombe, John Swan, J.W. Powell, and others that pieces from Ninstints families went to Chicago, New York, Ottawa, Victoria, and elsewhere. The computer-assisted cataloguing of museum collections, now underway around the world, may one day help in the rediscovery and reassemblage of the collections of artifacts that survive from this remarkable village.

About 1860 a child was born at Ninstints village who would eventually inherit the title of head chief. Given the Christian name of Tom Price, the young man moved with his family from the ancestral village to the more central and populous village of Skidegate about 1875. Price served as an informant on Kunghit Haida culture to a series of anthropologists at the turn of the century, most notably to Charles F. Newcombe of Victoria. Many of the geographical names, village locations, household lists, and legends were preserved for posterity through Tom Price's collaboration with the anthropologists.

Price's move to Skidegate brought him into contact with an accomplished group of argillite

Fig. 63 Tom Price. PAC, ca. 1900

carvers, from whom he gained a supply of the rare black-slate carving material. Price began to carve the ancient legends of his people, recording permanently in graphic form the struggles and achievements of their mythic heroes. He carved a wide variety of forms, from pipes to bowls, platters, and miniature totem poles. His specialty was the oval and circular platters on which he best captured the legends of the Ninstints people. Next to Charles Edenshaw, Price is the most narrative of all Haida argillite carvers. In addition to his argillite works, Price also carved in silver and in wood, including an interior pole for one of the chiefs of Tanu which has recently been added to the collection of the National Museum of Man.

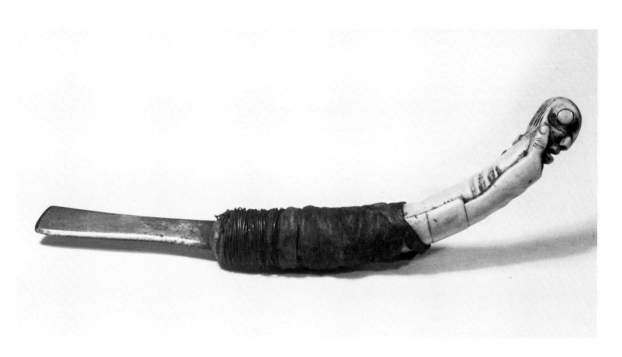

Fig. 64 *Knife from the village of Ninstints. NMC*

Fig. 65 *Copper from the village of Ninstints. NMC*

Fig. 66 *Painted design on a Haida Hat attributed to Tom Price UBCMOA (B. McLennan),* 1983

In his carvings, and in his two-dimensional paintings, Price displayed a distinctive personal interpretation of the conventional features of Kunghit Haida art. For this reason, his works are easily identified, even though they are unsigned. An aspect that he shares in common with other Ninstints carvers is the emphasis he placed on the upper part of the face, especially the eyes and eyebrows. One personal feature of his style was the prominence of the V-shape, around which his two-dimensional figures were organized. The use of a V-shape to represent the cleft in the forehead of crest animals is found throughout Haida art. Crest figures are created by attaching two profile animals at the nose and upper lip, or sometimes at the lower lip, which creates an inevitable cleft forehead. Price drove this cleft deeper into the animal's face, partly by enlarging the eyes and ears, which fall above the juncture point at the nose; this makes the V-form appear larger. He accentuated it even further by continuing the split into the arched bodies of the animals in their right and left profile, particularly in killer whales with their high dorsal fins. Since his own crest was the five-finned killer whale, early experimentation with killer whales may have prompted him in this direction. Two additional stylistic features which add emphasis to Tom Price's distinctive crest images are his tilting of the mouth line and eyes to complement the forehead V-shape. The eyes of the figure are pitched down towards the juncture point at the bridge of the nose, and the mouth is rendered as a very broad V-shape. Other formlines about the face, the eyebrow, and cheeklines are similarly treated, giving the entire face of the figure an upward thrust in two divergent planes, and a consequent sense of dynamism.

Fig. 67 & 68 Argillite plate attributed to Tom Price [above, VM(H. Tabbers), 1983] and a pencil drawing of a sea grizzly bear attributed to Tom Price (BCPM).

Tom Price played an active ceremonial role among his villagers at Skidegate, in addition to which he was a constable in his adopted village. On his death in 1927 the chiefly line of Ninstints was not formally assumed by a successor and passed into oblivion with the other names of the chiefs of Ninstints.

Fig. 69 Pencil drawing of a skate attributed to Tom Price. Note the exaggerated V-form of the head. BCPM

Fig. 70 Two-finned killer whale. Pencil drawing attributed to Tom Price. BCPM

Protecting the Heritage of Ninstints

The first steps to protect the heritage of Ninstints began when Charles Newcombe made a thorough photographic inventory of the village between 1897 and 1913. His sketch maps and notes of identification of monuments and houses amplify the rich record that forms the baseline for studies of this village. Newcombe was unable to collect actual monuments from the village because of its remoteness, but he did collect many of the items that had been brought from the village by the last inhabitants. He also collected works created later at Skidegate and Victoria by refugee artists such as Tom Price.

Although a few poles had been removed from Ninstints in 1938 and taken to Prince Rupert, serious efforts to salvage monuments from the village did not begin until after the Second World War. In 1947 Marius Barbeau led a National Museum of Man expedition which visited most of the Haida villages of the Queen Charlotte Islands, including Ninstints. The aim of that survey was to record the carvings photographically, to determine what could be saved, and to begin negotiations with the Haida descendants of the original owners regarding removal of pieces from their ancestral house sites. Barbeau also conceived the first plan to salvage the monuments themselves, as part of his extensive efforts to rescue totem poles and other monuments throughout the coast. His plan coincided with the interest of Harry B. Hawthorn of the Department of Anthropology and Sociology at U.B.C. and his wife, Audrey Hawthorn, then curator of the U.B.C. Museum of Anthropology.

Wilson Duff, who was curator of anthropology at the Provincial Museum of British Columbia from 1950 to 1965, made a brief reconnaissance of Ninstints in 1956, and in the following year he arranged to purchase from Haida descendants a number of Ninstints poles that could be salvaged and preserved. Through the initiative and support of Walter C. Koerner of Vancouver, a major salvage operation was then launched by the University of British Columbia and the Provincial Museum, led by Harry Hawthorn and including Duff, Michael Kew and John Smyly of the Provincial Museum, Wayne Suttles of the University of British Columbia, Bill Reid, the famous Haida artist who was then working for the C.B.C., and Bernard Atkins, photographer and film producer.

The first accurate map of Ninstints was produced during this 1957 expedition, drawn by John Smyly under the supervision of Wilson Duff. It recorded the location of every monument and house in the village in relation to major geographical features of the site.

The first archaeology at Ninstints was conducted by Suttles, now of the Portland State University , and Kew, now of U.B.C., who dug three test pits on the village site. The first test pit was inside the floor area of House 1. The second and third pits were in part of and just behind House 7. This was the deepest portion of the site and showed cultural deposits down to a depth of 2.1 metres, at which level the test excavation had to be abandoned because of lack of time. At the northern end of the site, from Houses 14 to 17, the deposit under the houses is very shallow, only a few centimetres of scattered shell debris, showing that the village was extended into this area in the latter part of the eighteenth century.

Tests to the south of the village indicated that the ground was cultivated by the inhabitants for potatoes and other crops introduced to the Haida by European traders in the late 1700's. Although aboriginal style artifacts were rare in the midden deposits at the village, numerous fragments of traded objects were found including glass beads, pieces of crockery and fragments of iron pots.

Fig. 71 Iron trade pot collected at Ninstints, showing evidence of native repair. UBCMOA (B. McLennan), 1983

Fig. 72 Crating sections of poles for shipment during 1957 expedition. BCPM (B. Atkins), 1957

Further archaeological tests were conducted in burial caves near the village. Whale bone in surprising abundance was noted in the cave deposits, although it probably represented material scavenged from whales which floated ashore on the island, since the Haida, unlike the Nootkan-speaking tribes of Vancouver Island, did not hunt whale.

The burial caves showed evidence of recent vandalism. Where there should have been decorated burial chests containing the remains of all but the noble classes of Ninstints, whose remains were installed in the mortuary posts, there were only scattered bone remains, along with fragments of the cedar bark matting and ropes with which the burial bundles were once enveloped. The most exciting find in the burial cave was the remains of a wooden mask which appears to represent a bear, of which the jaw and a portion of the face is preserved.

Fig. 73 One of the caves at Ninstints.
B.C. Ministry of Tourism, 1980

The major result of the 1957 expedition from a conservation point of view was the recovery of all or parts of twenty-three sculptured monuments, and a rich record of photography, films and notes. Seven of these poles are now in the Museum of Anthropology at U.B.C. They include two interior poles (from Houses 1 and 17), one mortuary pole (15X1), and four frontal poles (Houses 1, 9, 12, and 14). Three other poles which had originally gone to Victoria, plus two poles from Prince Rupert, were sent to the Queen Charlotte Islands Museum at Second Beach, the site of ancient Pebble Town, in 1975. A fire broke out in one of the Q.C.I. Museum sheds where paint was being removed from the poles, and all of the Ninstints poles were lost. Another pole was transferred from the B.C.P.M. to the Museum of Archaeology and Ethnology at Simon Fraser University.

On the basis of the material and information they had collected, Wilson Duff urged the provincial government to declare the site a provincial park. Ninstints had never been set aside as an Indian reserve because so few of the inhabitants of the village survived. It was rarely used after it was deserted, even on a seasonal basis, because it was so far from the new home of its former inhabitants. The site was declared a Provincial Park in 1958.

In the decades that followed a number of individuals visited the site to add elements to the existing records. I made several trips in the late 1960's and early 1970's to refine details of the Duff and Kew maps and to take colour photographs and film for the new galleries of the National Museum of Man in Ottawa.

In 1977 the Heritage Conservation Branch of the Office of the Provincial Secretary of British Columbia, along with conservation personnel at the B.C.P.M. under Richard Beauchamp, launched a series of studies aimed at long-term measures to safeguard what remained at the site. Photographic studies and sketches were made of each piece, and a detailed map of the house remains was made. The islets and foreshore of Anthony Island were declared an Ecological Reserve by the Provincial Government in 1979, and the island was designated a Provincial Archaeological and Heritage Site in the spring of 1980.

By 1980 a long term management plan had been worked out for the site, and the village was proposed by the Federal Government of Canada through its representative, Peter Bernett, to the World Heritage Site List of UNESCO on behalf of the Province of British Columbia. On 27 November 1981 Ninstints was declared "a World Heritage Site, of importance to the History of Mankind," by the UNESCO committee in Sydney, Australia.

Will Science Save Ninstints?

The declaration of Ninstints as a World Heritage Site initiated a new phase of interest in the long-term preservation of the site. Although the totem pole rescue project of 1957 under Harry Hawthorn had virtually written off the remaining monuments at Ninstints as being too far deteriorated to warrant the effort of recovery, it now became crucial to reassess the value of what was left at the site and to use modern scientific methods of analysis and preservation to save what remained. In the new perspective that followed UNESCO's decision that Ninstints was a significant site to the heritage of all mankind, every monument, no matter how ravaged by time and moisture, had to be assessed and to have its life prolonged as much as possible. Canada had made very rapid progress over the past decade in establishing the most advanced conservation laboratories in the world for the preservation of wooden heritage objects, both in Ottawa at the Canadian Conservation

Institute of the National Museums of Canada and the conservation laboratories of Parks Canada, and in Victoria at the British Columbia Provincial Museum.

The first objective of this research was to develop an accurate, up-to-date record of the site to support the submission to UNESCO. Following this, the researchers examined a host of factors relative to rates of deterioration and site conditions which could lead to the development of a long-term management plan that would ensure that a significant portion of the site was preserved for the education and enjoyment of native peoples, scholars, and the public.

The first accurate and detailed instrument survey of the site was done at this time by Ray Bonner, a surveyor with British Columbia's Ministry of Lands, Parks, and Housing. In that survey trees were cut to establish lines of sight the length and breadth of the village and the fallen monuments and timbers were cleared of moss and brush by a B.C.P.M. team under Richard Beauchamp to reveal their preserved outlines. Every fragment of the original structures was mapped and catalogued in this survey, and numbers were assigned to the monuments.

In the moist, high-latitude forest of the Queen Charlotte Islands, fallen trees become nurse logs to airborne seeds and are soon covered by a profusion of evergreen seedlings. Removal of hundreds of these seedlings firmly rooted in a fallen house timber or totem pole can be a frustrating and time-consuming affair. Random and careless removal of seedlings in the past by occasional visitors to the site who wanted to reveal obscured carvings on fallen poles often resulted in whole sections of the carving being ripped off the pole with the root mass of the current growth. Irreparable damage was done to fallen poles in many Haida village sites in this fashion.

Fig. 74 *The root of a seedling growing in the bottom section of this pole has been severed to prevent further growth, but the dead root system has been left in place, since removal would further damage the pole. B.C. Ministry of Tourism, 1980*

Clearing the site for the survey was followed by further cleaning of the monuments by conservators to reveal their details and to prevent further damage from the action of root growth into the old wood. Since plants retain moisture that is harmful to old wood, the removal of vegetation also served to dry the monuments and prolong their life expectancy.

The conservators at Ninstints carefully clipped, snipped, and sawed the vegetation and exposed roots from the poles in 1978 and 1979. The environmental surveys of Ninstints under Mary-Lou Florian and Richard Hebda of the B.C.P.M. sought to list the species of plants, shrubs, and trees on the village site and to assess the influence of vegetation on the deterioration of the poles. Some roots were left cut at the top and ring-barked at the bottom. Some were removed after careful consideration of the effect they would have when they rotted and fell off, perhaps carrying chunks of the pole with them.

In conjunction with the environmental work at the site, Florian conducted background studies on the poles outside the U.B.C. Museum of Anthropology that had been carved in recent years by Bill Reid. She found that if kept clear of vegetation and moisture, western red cedar, of which the poles were carved, would allow for great longevity. This is confirmed by the study of the survival rate of exposed wood in ancient Japanese temples. In fact, one of the more serious threats to the surface of the carvings revealed in one study was the removal of cellulose fibres from the surface of the poles by wasps to build their nests.

Using a wide range of photographs taken over some eight decades on the site, Florian established a file for each of the Ninstints monuments that documents the progress of vegetation growth. Analysis of these individual monument records provided many insights into why the poles are in the condition they are today as well as ideas for the future protection of carved monuments under the environmental conditions of the Queen Charlotte Islands.

In the summer of 1981 Don Abbott, an archaeologist from the B.C.P.M., excavated the base of a frontal pole and a mortuary pole in order to assess the rate and nature of decay. Neither excavation could be completed to the bottom of the stump since large rocks used to support the poles inhibited the efforts of the diggers. The frontal pole, that of House 14, extended more than the deepest probe to 1.45 metres below the surface. The mortuary pole, 12x, went deeper than the maximum excavation to 0.80 metres below the surface.

Fig. 75 Eighteen trees obscuring the poles at Ninstints were felled in 1982 by Tom Greene, a Haida from Skidegate. V. Husband

Fig. 76 Side plate of a musket excavated at Ninstints. BCPM (B. McLennan), 1983

The dating of objects found in the fill around the mortuary pole, including parts of a musket and a plate from the Crystal Palace in London, indicate a date not earlier than the 1850's and not later than the 1880's. Thus, this pole may have been one of the last erected at Ninstints. In addition, there was a curious cache of two wood-cutting adzes, placed behind the frontal pole at the ground surface on either side of the entrance to the house. The blade of one adze was of metal, but the other was of stone and of advanced Indian manufacture. At present-day Haida pole-raising ceremonies the carvers dance around the poles with their adzes and carving tools strung around their neck. It appears that a similar cere-mony may have been held at Ninstints, after which the adzes were deposited behind the pole.

In the summer of 1982 at the request of the B.C.P.M., a specialized study of the condition of the remaining monuments began with the arri-val at Ninstints of a recording crew from the Canadian Conservation Institute of the Nation-al Museum of Canada in Ottawa under David Gratton. Selected poles were x-rayed to deter-mine the density, and hence strength, of the re-maining poles. The contact zone of the base of the pole was sheathed in sensitive film and an x-ray camera was mounted in stations around the base to bombard the pole and record the tree-ring densities on the film target behind. The analysis of this data was processed through a computer at the Conservation Institute.

In terms of future archaeological study the swampy area at the north end of the village behind Houses 14–17 appears to hold the greatest potential. Whereas excessive moisture is respon-sible for much of the decay of monuments at Ninstints, if wooden and fibrous remains are permanently submerged in a wet environment then decay is slowed and long-term preservation is ensured. Elsewhere on the coast of B.C. sites have been found in swampy or tidal areas with wooden artifacts as much as 3,000 years old in an excellent state of preservation. It is impossible to predict what flesh these future finds could put on the bones of the Ninstints monuments, but the potential of the site is exciting.

Selected Readings

Acheson, Steve
  1979   "To Illustrate a Management Proposal for Anthony Island." Report on file, Office of the Provincial Archaeologist, Victoria.
  1980   "Ninstints Village." *Datum.* Victoria, B.C.: Ministry of the Provincial Secretary & Government Services, Spring, pp. 13-17.
Barbeau, Charles Marius
  1950   *Totem Poles.* 2, vols. Ottawa: Queen's Printer.
Bartlett, John
  1925   A narrative of events in the life of John Bartlett of Boston, Mass., in the years 1790-1793, during voyages to Canton and the northwest coast of North America. Detached from *The Sea, the Ship, and the Sailor.* Salem, Mass.: Marine Research Society.
Beauchamp, Richard
  1978   "A Work Report on Ninstints Village, Anthony Island, May 18th-25th, 1979." Unpublished B.C.P.M. manuscript.
  1979   "A Work Report on Ninstints Village, Anthony Island, May 26th-June 1st, 1978." Unpublished B.C.P.M. manuscript.
Bishop, Charles
  1794-96 "Journal of the Ship Ruby, 1794-6." Typescript copy in Provincial Archives of British Columbia.
Chittenden, N.H.
  1884   *Exploration of the Queen Charlotte Islands.* Victoria, B.C.
Collison, W.H.
  1915   *In the Wake of the War Canoe.* London. Reprinted. Vancouver: Douglas & MacIntyre.
Dawson, G.M.
  1880   "Report on the Queen Charlotte Islands." Geological Survey of Canada, Report of Progress for 1878-79. Ottawa.
Deans, James
  1899   "Tales from the Totems of the Hidery." O.L. Triggs, ed., Arch. Int. Folk-lore Assoc., vol. 2, Chicago.
Duff, Wilson & Michael Kew
  1957   "Anthony Island, A Home of the Haidas." B.C. Provincial Museum. *Annual Report,* pp. 37-64.
Florian, Mary-Lou E., Richard Beauchamp, and Barbara Kennedy.
  1982   *Haida Totem Pole Conservation: Ninstints Village, Anthony Island, British Columbia.* Proceedings of the ICOMOS Wood Committee IV International Symposium, 1982.
Howay, F.W.
  1920   "The Voyage of the Hope: 1790-1792." *Washington Historical Quarterly* 11, pp. 3-28.
  1925   "Indian Attacks upon Maritime Traders of the Northwest Coast, 1785-1805." *Canadian Historical Review* 6, pp. 287-309.

1929   "The Ballad of the Bold Northwestman: An Incident in the Life of Captain John Kendrick." *Washington Historical Quarterly* 20, pp. 114–23.   *102*

1941   "Voyages of the 'Columbia' to the Northwest Coast, 1787–1790 and 1790–1793." Boston: Massachusetts Historical Society.

Ingraham, Joseph
1792   "Journal of the Voyage of the Brigatine 'Hope'." Typescript in Provincial Archives of British Columbia.

MacDonald, George F.
1983   *Haida Monumental Art: The Villages of the Queen Charlotte Islands.* Vancouver: University of B.C. Press.

Newcombe, C.F.
1897   Manuscript on file with the British Columbia Provincial Museum.

Poole, Francis
1872   *Queen Charlotte Islands: A Narrative of Discovery and Adventure in the North Pacific.* London.

Swanton, John R.
1909   "Contributions to the Ethnology of the Haida." *Memoir of the American Museum of Natural History,* vol. 5.

Films about Ninstints

Ninstints. Spreitz-Husband Productions, 1983.
The Silent Ones. Government of B.C. Production, 1957.
Totem. Canadian Broadcasting Corporation Prod., 1957.

Photographic Credits

The following individuals and institutions have given permission to reproduce photographs used in this volume:

British Columbia Provincial Archives (BCPA)
British Columbia Provincial Museum (BCPM)
V. Husband
G. Miller
National Museums Canada (NMC)
Province of British Columbia, Ministry of Tourism
————, Ministry of Environment
Public Archives Canada (PAC)
K. Spreitz
University of British Columbia Museum of Anthropology (UBCMOA)
Vancouver Museum (VM)